GREAT WOMEN IN AMERICAN HISTORY

2nd Grade U.S. History Vol 5

Speedy Publishing LLC
40 E. Main St. #1156
Newark, DE 19711
www.speedypublishing.com

Women have contributed significantly to American history.

DEBORAH MOODY

1586 – 1659

brought settlers seeking religious freedom to Gravesend at New Amsterdam. She was the first female landowner in the New World.

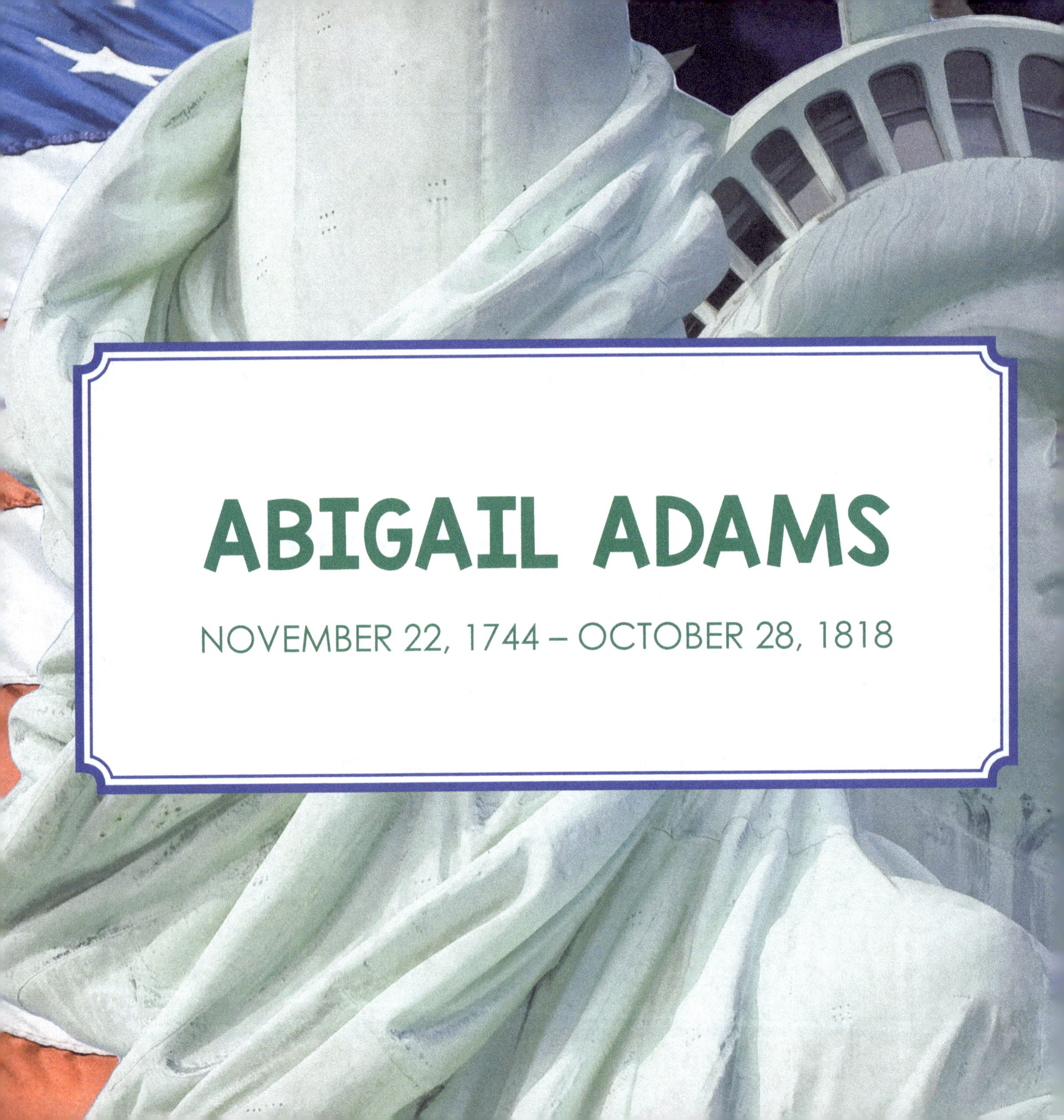

ABIGAIL ADAMS

NOVEMBER 22, 1744 – OCTOBER 28, 1818

was the wife of President John Adams, mother of President John Quincy Adams. In one of her letters Abigail asked John to "Remember the ladies". This became a famous quote used by women's rights leaders for years to come.

SUSAN B. ANTHONY

FEBRUARY 15, 1820 – MARCH 13, 1906

was an American social reformer and feminist. She was called "the Napoleon" of the women's movement, she spent 60 years leading the fight for suffrage.

CLARA BARTON

DECEMBER 25, 1821 – APRIL 12, 1912

was a pioneering nurse who founded the American Red Cross. She was called “the angel of the battlefield” for her ministrations during the Civil War.

AMELIA EARHART

JULY 24, 1897 – disappeared JULY 2, 1937

was an American aviation pioneer and author. She was the first woman to fly solo across the Atlantic Ocean. Earhart was received back in the United States as a hero.

HELEN KELLER

JUNE 27, 1880 – JUNE 1, 1968

was an American author and lecturer. She was the first deafblind person to earn a bachelor of arts degree. She campaigned for women's suffrage, labor rights, socialism, and other similar causes.

ROSA PARKS

FEBRUARY 4, 1913 – OCTOBER 24, 2005

was an African-American Civil Rights activist. The United States Congress called her "the first lady of civil rights". Her refusal to give up her seat sparked the Montgomery Bus Boycott of 1955.

SALLY RIDE

MAY 26, 1951 – JULY 23, 2012

was an American physicist and astronaut. She joined NASA in 1978 and became the first American woman in space in 1983.

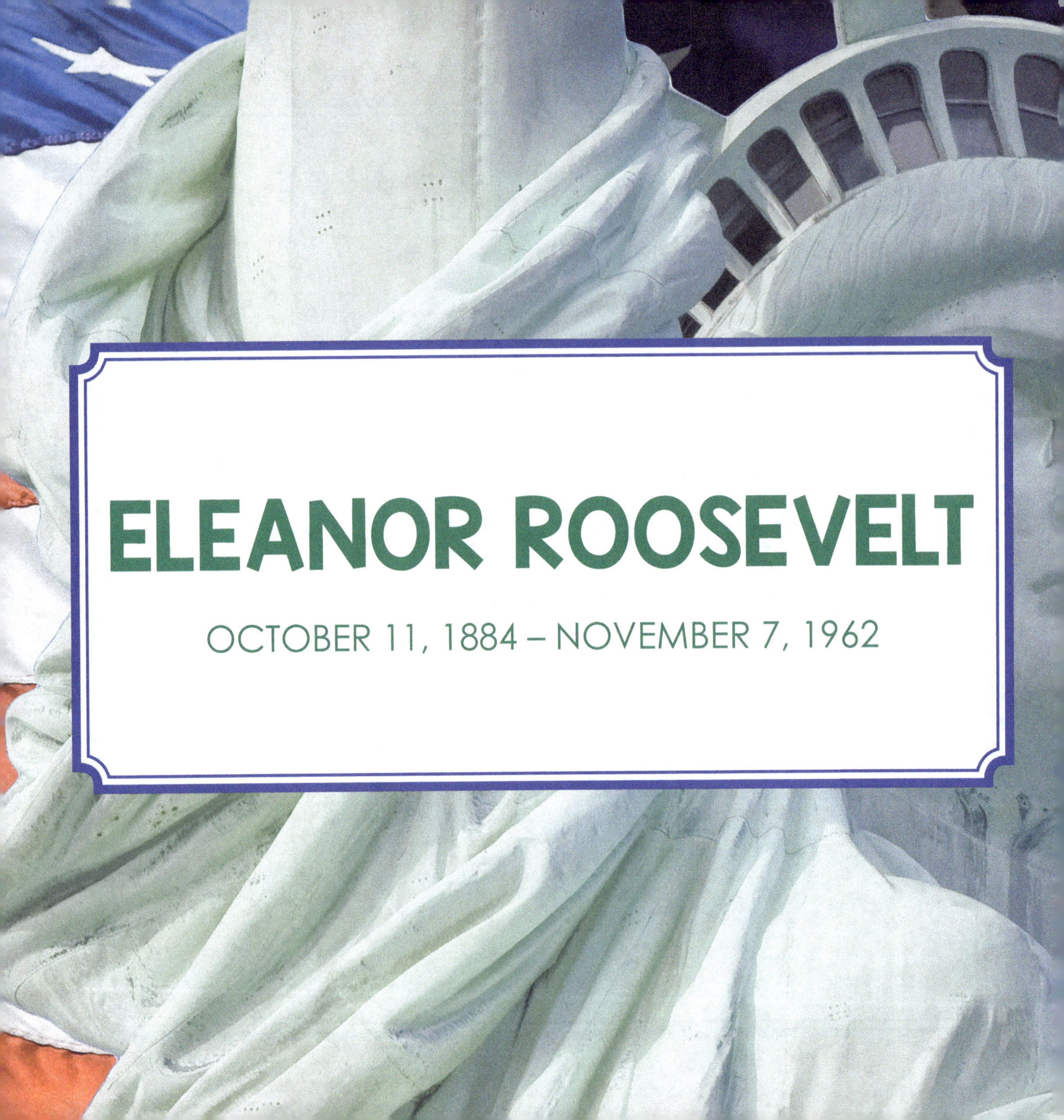

ELEANOR ROOSEVELT

OCTOBER 11, 1884 – NOVEMBER 7, 1962

was an American politician and activist. She supported the United Nations and was directly involved in the drafting of the Universal Declaration of Human Rights.

HARRIET BEECHER STOWE

JUNE 14, 1811 – JULY 1, 1896

was an American abolitionist and author. She is best known for her novel Uncle Tom's Cabin that changed forever the public perception of slavery. It depicts the harsh life for African Americans under slavery.

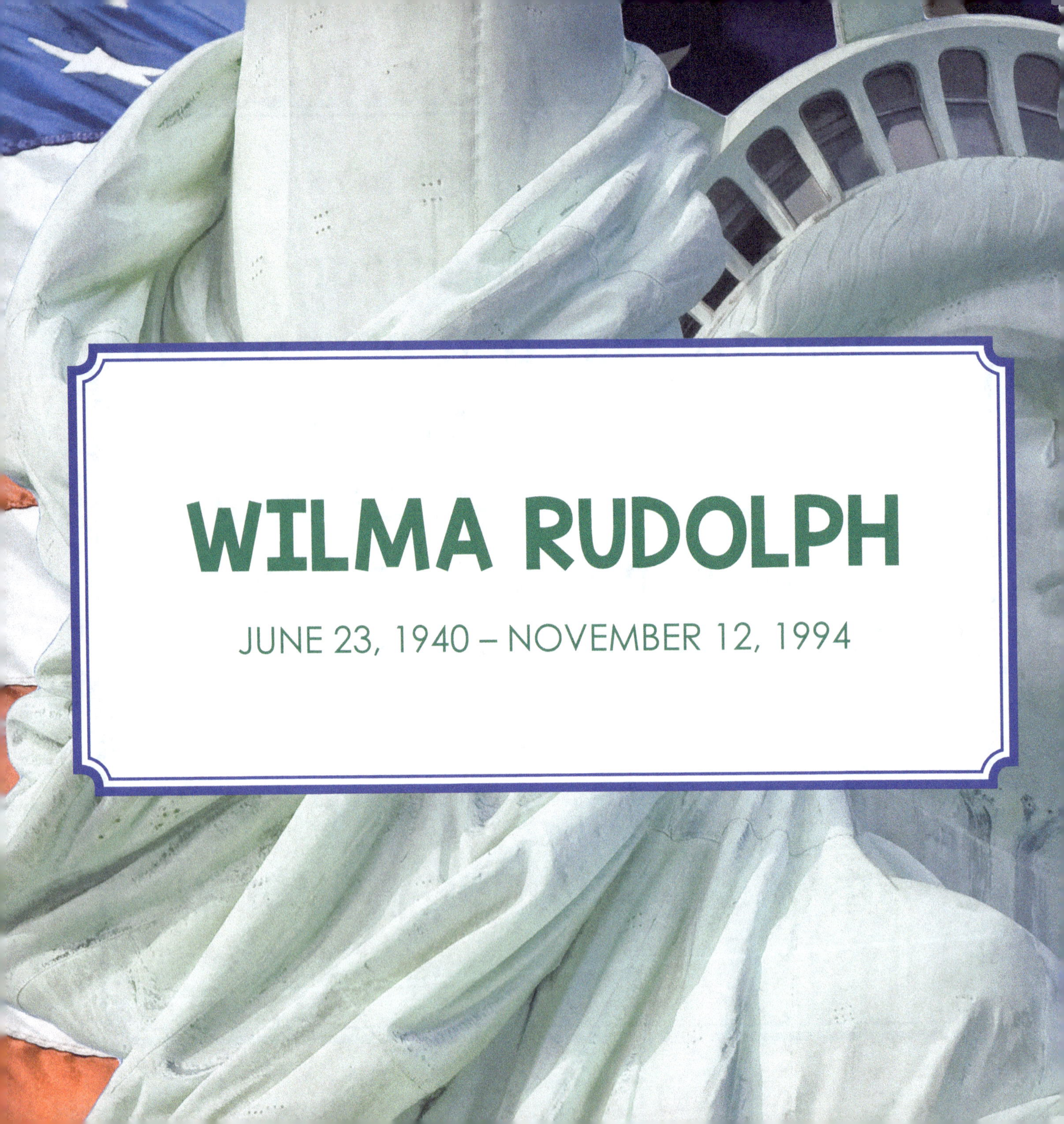

WILMA RUDOLPH

JUNE 23, 1940 – NOVEMBER 12, 1994

was an American track and field sprinter. Rudolph became the first American woman to win three gold medals in track and field during a single Olympic Games.

GRACE HOPPER

DECEMBER 9, 1906 – JANUARY 1, 1992

was an American computer scientist. She is the inventor of the compiler, which made modern computer programming possible. She is credited with popularizing the term "debugging" for fixing computer glitches.

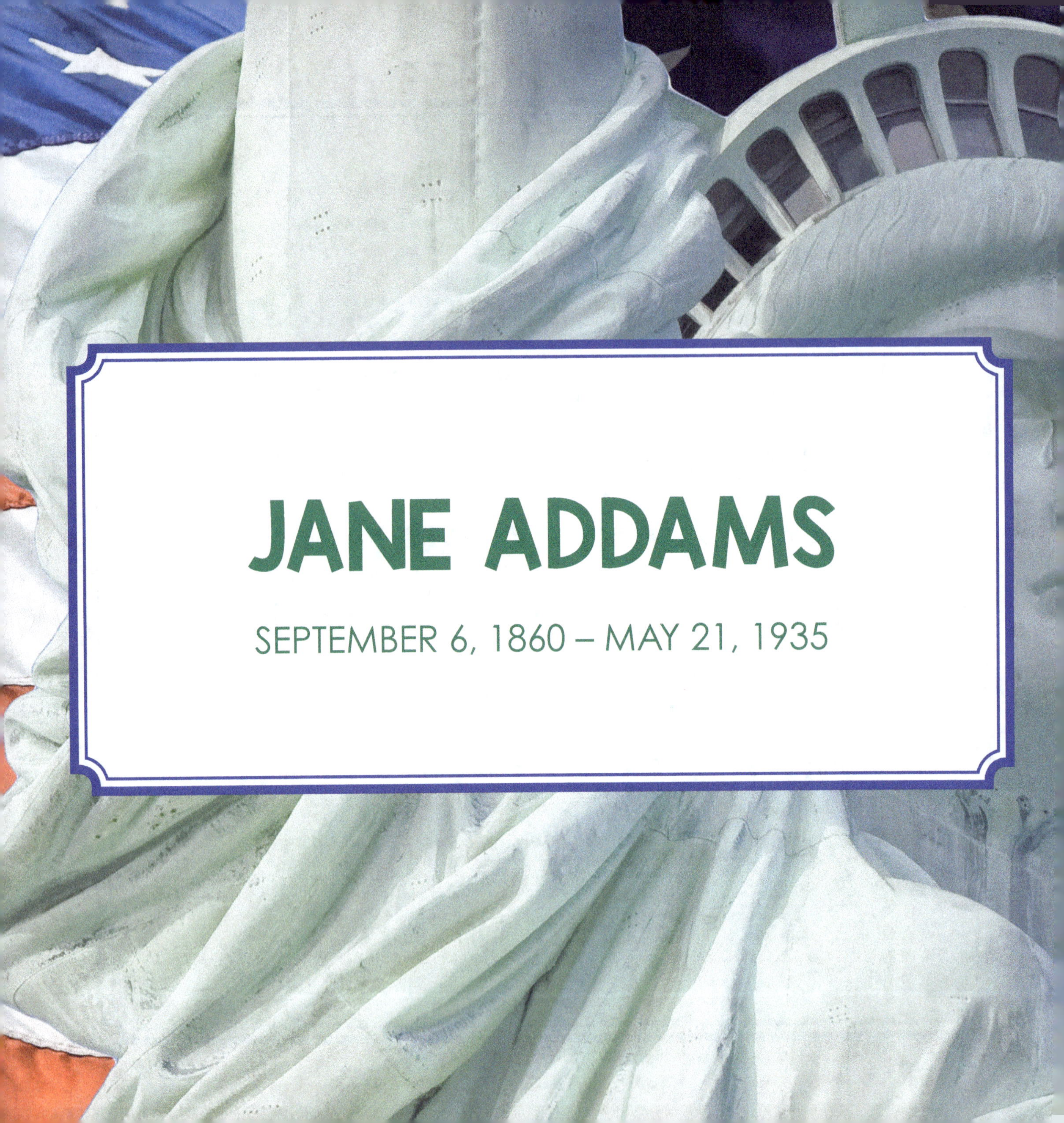

JANE ADDAMS

SEPTEMBER 6, 1860 – MAY 21, 1935

was a pioneer American settlement activist and leader in women's suffrage and world peace. She is the founder of Hull House and became the second woman to win the Nobel Prize for Peace.

FLORENCE BASCOM

JULY 14, 1862 – JUNE 18, 1945

was an American geologist. The first woman and female geologist to earn a Ph.D. from Johns Hopkins. She became the first woman hired by the United States Geological Survey.

PEARL S. BUCK

JUNE 26, 1892 – MARCH 6, 1973

was an American writer and novelist. Author of books reflecting her life in China. She was the first woman to win the Nobel Prize in Literature.

ELIZABETH BLACKWELL

FEBRUARY 3, 1821 – MAY 31, 1910

was the first woman to receive a medical degree in the United States. She opened a slum infirmary and trained women in medicine.

RACHEL CARSON

MAY 27, 1907 – APRIL 14, 1964

was an American marine biologist, conservationist and the author of Silent Spring. Carson was the founding mother of the modern environmental movement.

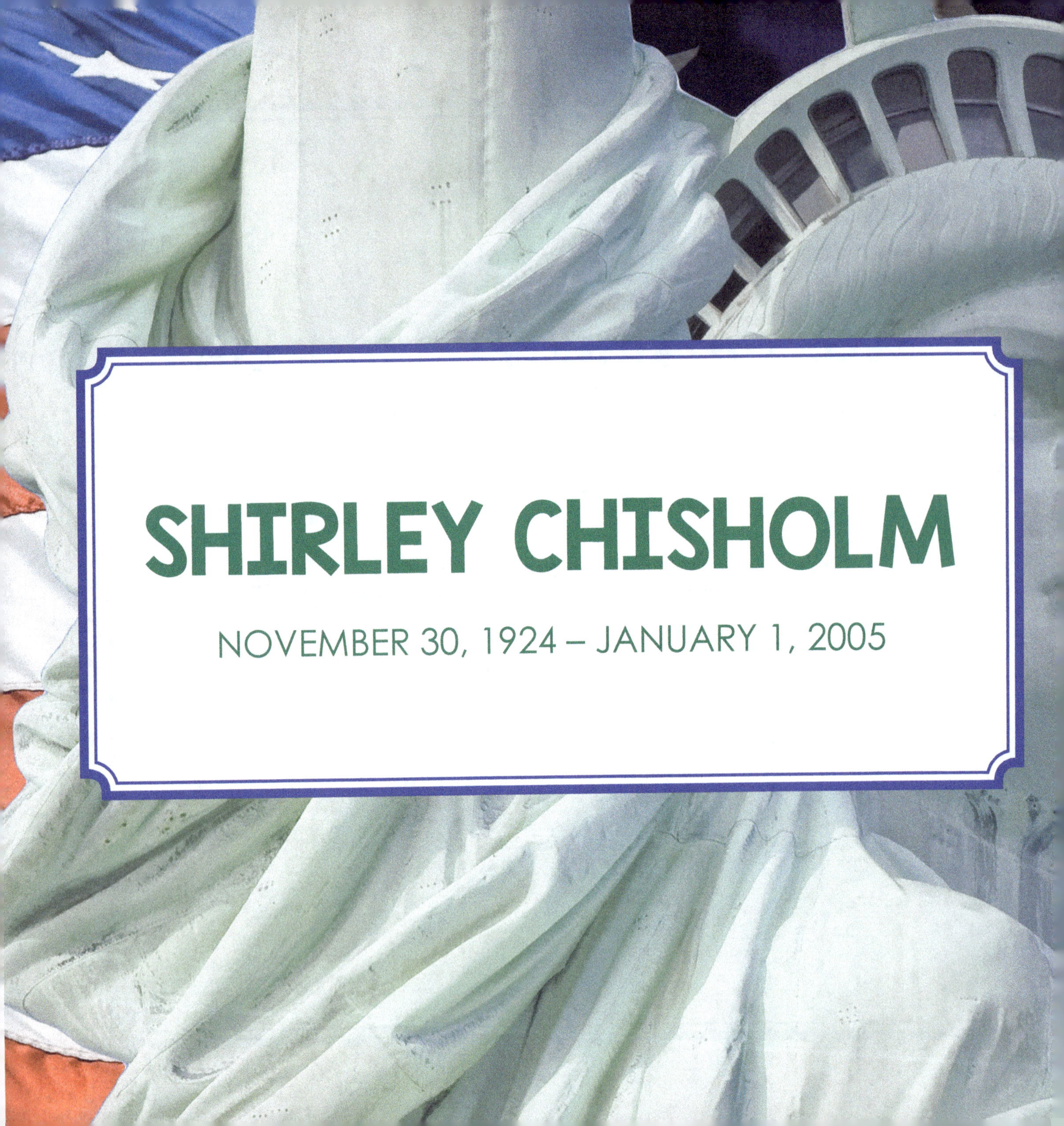

SHIRLEY CHISHOLM

NOVEMBER 30, 1924 – JANUARY 1, 2005

was an American politician and author. She was the first black woman elected to the United States Congress (1968). She became the first woman ever to run for the Democratic presidential nomination.

Visit
BABY PROFESSOR
EDUCATION KIDS
www.BabyProfessorBooks.com
to download Free Baby Professor eBooks
and view our catalog of new and exciting
Children's Books

www.ingramcontent.com/pod-product-compliance
Lightning Source LLC
LaVergne TN
LVHW060831170826
845678LV00010B/1951

* 9 7 9 8 8 6 9 4 4 9 1 0 8 *